102 SLANG WORDS AND EXPRESSIONS IN SPANISH FROM SPAIN

Learn the 102 most-used
Slang words and Expressions
in Spanish from Spain with
21 real-life dialogues

by
Digital Polyglot

CONTENTS

Title Page

Introduction   1

Content structure   4

How should I read this book?   6

Glossary   8

EL DILEMA DE MARTA   105

Characters   106

Marta   107

Raquel   108

Laura   109

Carlos   110

Luís   111

Introduction to the story   112

1. Laura es una borde   113

2. Un finde no muy tranqui   116

3. Los cabrones de recursos humanos   118

4. Raquel es una máquina   121

5. Unos frikis muy majos   123

6. No tan mal después de todo   126

7. Marta se mete en un marrón   129

8. Vaya Laura   131

9. Marta se encabrona   133

10. Los papeleos de siempre   135

11. Lana de alpaca pija   137

12. El Luís es muy majo   140

13. Me puse de los nervios   142

14. Fin del papeleo   144

15. Todo va a salir de lujo   146

16. La pava de Laura otra vez   148

17. Flipando con el nuevo proyecto   150

18. Marta sí que va a saco   152

19. Noche de cotilleo   154

20. No me llaman, qué putada   156

21. Todo tiene su final   158

THANKS FOR READING!   161

About Digital Polyglot   162

Join the club!   163

Introduction

Let's be honest: How much of the Spanish you have learned at school do you actually use in your day-to-day life? Doesn't it frustrate you to invest so many hours in something you're not going to put into practice? Understanding the subjunctive is fine, but if you can't express yourself fluently it isn't worth the pain.

Have you tried following a conversation in Spanish? Chances are, you didn't understand much. This is because Spaniards use a lot of slang and expressions in their daily conversations, which they probably didn't teach you at school. This doesn't mean that the Spanish they teach you at school is a waste of time, but if you want to understand the authentic Spanish, the one that is spoken on a daily basis, you need something else...

That's why we bring you this book. We believe

that informal language is an important part of language learning, especially when it comes to Spanish language, and in order to help you with that we have compiled the 102 most used slang words and expressions in everyday Spanish of the new decade (2020's). Unlike your school, we haven't omitted the bad words, as they are also part of the colloquial language. Our everyday life is full of emotions that evoke a language rich in curse words that you also have to learn.

Not only that. We know that like every language lover you are also curious, that's why we have done an exhaustive research work to bring you the origin of each word, and thus help you understand the history behind each one of them. You will be surprised, for example, to find out where the word 'cabrearse' comes from (spoiler alert: It does not come from the word 'cabrón'), and that 'de puta madre' means something totally different from 'tu puta madre'. We have also provided very practical examples so that you understand how each word should be used, and variations, in case the word can be used differently.

We know that it's not enough that you know the words and their origin, it's very important to know how they are applied in an everyday conversation too. That is why we bring you the story of Marta, a brave girl from Galicia who moved to Barcelona in search of new challenges. In this story you will learn exactly how each word should be used in the form of very natural and fun dialogues. Marta's story has been written entirely in Spanish from Spain, so you really know how Spaniards speak in their day-to-day.

"102 Slang words and Expressions" is the perfect complement to your Spanish course. When you finish reading this book you will be able to understand what your Spanish friends really say and you will even be able to answer them; you cannot imagine the surprise they will get. With this you will develop your confidence and it will be much easier for you to express yourself in an informal context.

Content structure

In order to explain each word in detail and how to use them, we have structured the content as follows:

Definition: Many words have more than one meaning. We will put the most frequent meaning first and the secondary ones later.

Origin: We have done our best to investigate the origin of each word. Unfortunately not all the words have a clear origin, so for those ones we have tried to give a logical explanation based on its etymology.

Use: We will detail the most precise way to use the words, the contexts in which they should be used, whether you can use it in all contexts or only with close friends; and even other words that could be used instead.

Examples: Examples are the best way to learn anything. We have put examples from real life so that whenever you have to apply what you have learned you will do it with accuracy and you can camouflage yourself among the natives.

Variations: Many words can be used in different ways depending on the context. We have put the most relevant variations, although there is something very important to keep in mind:

There are many words that despite having the same root have very different meanings, for example the words 'petar' and 'petarlo': 'petar' means to explode or to break, while 'petarlo' means to succeed in a big way. As you can see, despite sharing the same root their meanings are very different, that's why 'petarlo' will not appear as a variation of 'petar' and will count as a new word. The opposite occurs with words like 'pasta' (money) and 'pastón' (money). They both share the same root but also have the same meaning so 'pastón' will appear as a variation of 'pasta' and not as a new word.

How should I read this book?

You're free to read this book the way you want. Nevertheless we've come up with two ways that might help you get the most out of the information on this book, depending on your level:

Following the glossary:

If you have a beginner/intermediate level you might want to start with the glossary making sure you understand the meaning of each word, and only then go to read the story to learn how to use them in context. You can always come back to the glossary to make sure you understand everything in the story.

Following the story:

If you have an intermediate/advanced level you might want to go directly to the story and go back to the glossary for understanding and more information about each word, its origin and use. Still we highly recommend you to read each word in the glossary since some words have different ways of use, plus very unexpected origins that you won't want to miss.

Are you ready to start this journey?

¡Dale caña!

Glossary

A saco

Definition: 'A saco' is an expression that is used to indicate that you have to go all out, do your best to carry out the action. You can also say "ir a full".

Origin: The origin of the expression 'A saco' is found in the verb 'saquear', which was the act that was carried out in the past, during periods of war, in which soldiers who invaded a place entered houses/dwellings/businesses and devastated with everything of value that they caught. For this they used large bags ('sacos') that they carried with them and in which they deposited the greatest number of things that they could steal.

That type of robbery became known as looting ('saqueo') and with it the expression 'entrar a saco' was born as a synonym for doing something in a disrespectful way, giving it over the years the different variants of use that we all know today.

Use: You can say 'ir a saco' or use any verb and

add 'a saco' at the end, such as 'trabajar a saco'.

Examples: "Tengo que trabajar a saco el domingo si quiero acabar el trabajo para el lunes".

Variations: Ir **a saco**, entrar **a saco**.

A tope

Definition: To the maximum, to the limit.

Origin: To find the origin of this expression we have to go to the nautical environments.

Carrying a ship loaded with excess merchandise or crew/passengers, in times when the space of the ship was used to the maximum in a voyage, gave rise to expressions such as 'ir a tope' or 'estar a tope' that ended up being used in colloquial language outside of marine environments.

Use: This expression is used to say that something or someone is at the limit of their abilities.

Examples: "Está trabajando a tope para intentar acabar a tiempo".

Variations: Ir **a tope**, estar **a tope**.

Apañarse

Definition: Fixing something. Managing to achieve something.

Origin: The word 'apañar' (clean, wipe) comes from a- + paño (wipe) + -ar. Maybe it's because of this that 'apañarse' is related to solving something or achieving something difficult.

Use: As it's a reflexive verb (apañar-se) it should be used with a reflexive pronoun.

Examples: "No te preocupes, **yo me apaño** solo".

Variations: N/A.

Birra

Definition: Beer.

Origin: This word comes from the Italian 'birra', which in turn comes from the Latin 'bibere', to drink.

Use: Normally to replace the word 'cerveza' in an informal context.

Examples: ¿Te parece si lo conversamos con unas **birras**?

Variations: N/A.

Borde

Definition: Someone that is rude and unpleasant to deal with.

Origin: The origin of borde is found in the Latin word burdus, which was used to refer to bastards (children born out of wedlock) and to those plants that sprouted without having been cultivated or grafted.

Several words were derived from the term burdus, including the aforementioned 'borde' to refer to someone impertinent or unpleasant; since it was believed that children born out of wedlock enjoyed this sour and dry character. 'Burdo', meaning coarse, crude, rude. Or the word 'burdel', as a reference to the place where the prostitutes sometimes had children -bastards- with some clients.

Use: It is mainly used to refer to a person who is not very delicate and therefore is disliked.

Examples: "No soporto a la Laura, es una **borde**, siempre está gritando".

Variations: N/A.

Botellón

Definition: A noisy and generally nocturnal meeting of young people, in which alcoholic beverages are consumed in abundance.

Origin: The word 'botellón' (large bottle) comes from the augmentative (-on) of 'botella' (bottle), since it's where alcoholic beverages are normally consumed.

Use: Generally used for outdoor gatherings although it can eventually be used for home gatherings.

Examples: Los chavales hicieron **botellón** en el parque central y lo dejaron asqueroso.

Variations: N/A.

Cabrearse

Definition: To get angry. To get really irritated.

Origin: The word 'cabrearse' comes from 'cabreo'. The 'cabreo', in its origin, was the demand to the peasants to pay a fee for the use of real or noble land.

The term "cabreo" or "cabrevación" emerged in the Middle Ages, in the time of Alfonso XI de Castilla (1311-1350), to designate the legal act of registering land or estates that were subject to the payment of royal or noble charges.

And how did the expression "cabrearse" become popular with the sense that we give it today of "severe anger"? This transfer is due to the conflict that was experienced in Spain in the 19th century between the peasantry and the nobility as a result of these 'cabrevaciones', especially in the northwest of Catalonia.

Most of the sentences were unfavorable to the 'campesinos cabreados'. It is not surprising, therefore, that they showed monumental anger at the authorities every time they were summoned to these procedural acts. And so the current meaning of "cabrearse", "cabreo" and "estar cabreado" emerged, which although it may seem otherwise has nothing to do with cabras (goats).

Use: It can be used in two ways, as an adjective, for example: "Ese tío está muy cabreado" or as a verb, for example "Me estoy cabreando con todo esto".

Examples: "Estoy **cabreado** con este tema de la cuarentena".

Variations: Cabreado.

Cabrón

Definition: Person of bad intention or character. Bad person.

Origin: The origin of this word is uncertain but one of the most frequent hypotheses is that in the past when shepherds spent too much time in the field, they used to have sexual relations with their goats, sheep and cows.

The word "cabrón" is given to the male goat (cabra macho) that witnesses how the shepherd has sexual relations with his females without being able to do anything. Perhaps that is why someone who's been cheated on is also called a 'cabrón'.

Use: Generally used to insult someone, but can also be used as a joke with close friends.

Examples: "Ese tío es un **cabrón**, mira adónde echa la basura", "Qué **cabrón**, te aumentan el sueldo y además te compras un coche nuevo".

Variations: Cabrona, cabronazo, cabroncete, cabroncillo, cabroncito.

Cagarla

Definition: Damage something.

Origin: 'Caca' means poop, so 'cagarla' literally translates to 'to shit it up'. The equivalent in English would be 'to screw it up'.

Use: It's used when you said or did something counterproductive. This expression is a bit vulgar, so it should only be used with people you know.

Examples: "Le puse mucho azúcar a la tarta, creo que **la cagué**".

Variations: N/A.

Cagarse en la leche

Definition: Expresses anger or irritation at something, indicating contempt.

Origin: The original expression was: "Me cago en la leche que mamaste", that means "I shit on the milk you sucked", giving to indicate contempt to the mother of whom is insulted, since it's very common to use the maternal figure to insult or curse. This phrase later became "Me cago en la leche", and now it's only used to curse.

Use: It should only be used with people you trust since it's a very vulgar expression. It's used to express a lot of anger.

Examples: "¡**Me cago en la leche**, este tío dejó los platos sucios de nuevo!".

Variations: N/A.

Caña

Definition: Glass of beer, generally of 330ml.

Origin: The name of the 'caña' comes from the tube through which the beer rises from the moment it comes out of the barrel until it comes out of the tap. This vertical tube or "caña" (word related to pipe) is the one that gives its name to the beer served through a tap.

Use: It can be used in any informal context.

Examples: "¡Dos **cañas** y una clara por favor!".

Variations: Cañita, cañilla.

Capullo

Definition: Naive, clumsy, inexperienced.

Origin: Capullo means 'cocoon', although it's uncertain how it started to be used to describe someone who is naive.

Use: It's used to say that someone is naive or stupid, it can be used with friends or strangers (if you want to have problems).

Examples: ¡Qué miras, tío **capullo**!

Variations: Capullín, capullito, capullete, capullazo.

Cebollazo

Definition: Drunkenness.

Origin: The word 'cebollazo' comes from 'cebolla' (onion) + 'azo' (augmentative) and it literally means 'hit by an onion'. The word 'cebollazo' is normally used to describe a hard hit, in this case the hard hit would be the hangover after the drunkenness.

Use: You can say 'pegar un cebollazo' or 'pillar un cebollazo'.

Examples: "Aquel finde me pegué un **cebollazo** que no recuerdo nada".

Variations: N/A.

Chalado

Definition: Crazy.

Origin: It comes from the word 'chalar' of origin Caló.

Use: It can be used in the same way that the word 'loco' (crazy).

Examples: "Ese Manolo es un **chalado**, se metió al mar en pleno invierno".

Variations: Chalar (to go crazy).

Chaval

Definition: Young person.

Origin: It comes from the Caló language.

Use: Used to call or speak to someone whose name is unknown. It's also used to call a friend.

Examples: "¡**Chaval**, no tires piedras a las ventanas!", "Bueno **chaval**, ¿Qué planes tenemos para hoy?".

Variations: Chavalito, chavalote, chavalillo, chavalete, chavalón.

Chiringuito

Definition: Kiosk or stall for drinks and simple meals outdoors.

Origin: According to the DRAE, 'chiringuito' means 'kiosk or outdoor drinks stall'.

This word is likely to have its origins in Cuba. They say that, during the 19th century, workers in sugar cane plantations had coffee when they stopped to rest. They took a stocking, filled it with coffee, and then poured water on it. The stocking was used as a strainer, used to filter the coffee.

So, the 'chorrito' (trickle) that came out of that stocking was called 'chiringo'. Over time, small kiosks of cane and leaves were created, and there the peasants rested and drank their coffee. "Let's go to the chiringuito," they said.

Use: It can be used in any informal situation. It is mostly used for food and drink stalls near the beach.

Examples: "Vamos a tomarnos unas cervezas al **chiringuito** de la esquina, ¿Te vienes?".

Variations: Chiringo.

Chorrada

Definition: Baloney, bullshit, nonsense, stupid action.

Origin: The origin goes back to the time when liquids were bought in bulk (wine, oil, milk...). It was the norm for the shopkeeper to dispense after the quantity requested (for example a quarter of a litre of wine) a small portion of the product (as a tip) which was known as 'chorrada'. But this extra small amount was usually so small that it was ridiculous and scarce, so everything that was of little value started to be called like that.

Use: It's used to refer to the little value of something or to point out that some nonsense or foolishness has been said.

Examples: "Me he comprado cuatro **chorradas**", "Déjate de **chorradas** y ponte a currar".

Variations: N/A.

Chulo

Definition: Very attractive or desirable thing or situation.

Origin: From Hispanic Arabic شل (šúlo).

Use: Used to describe something that is funny or that we like.

Examples: "Llevas un gorro muy **chulo**", "¡Qué **chulo** estuvo el espectáculo!".

Variations: Chulísimo, chulazo.

Chungo

Definition: Of poor appearance, quality or condition.

Origin: It comes from the Caló language which means 'ugly'.

Use: It's used to describe situations or things that do not look good. Also difficult or messy situations.

Examples: "Ha sido una semana muy **chunga**, me dejaron mucho trabajo".

Variations: N/A.

Chupito

Definition: Small serving of a strong alcoholic beverage. It's usually served in very small glasses and drunk in one gulp.

Origin: The origin of this word is uncertain but perhaps it comes from the word 'chupar' which means 'to suck', a rather informal way of saying 'to drink'. Being a very small portion, the diminutive '-ito' is used, thus obtaining the word 'chupito'.

The reason why alcohol began to be consumed in such small quantities was a result of the application of the Dry Act or Volstead Act in the United States. This law prohibited the manufacture, transport and sale of alcoholic products between 1920 and 1933 throughout the country. But once the law was passed, the trap was set, and soon after, illegal liquor stores, called speakeasies, sprang up. They forced the parishioners to drink very quickly and in small glasses, so that they would not be caught by the police if they broke into the premises.

Use: It can be used in any context, generally young people use it more often.

Examples: "Vamos por unos **chupitos** y luego a la discoteca".

Variations: N/A.

Churri

Definition: Loving way to call a partner or date.

Origin: The word 'churri' comes from the abbreviation of the word "pichurri", which is a nickname for a loving partner.

Currently the term 'churri' is used with various meanings, one of them to refer to the couple or girlfriend. However, it can also refer to other women/men who are not necessarily ones partner, for example: "Conocí a una churri muy simpática" (I met a very nice girl).

Use: It can be used in any informal situation. Usually to talk about someone's partner or to refer lovingly to their own partner.

Examples: "**Churri**, cariño! ¿Sigues ahí? ¡Sí, mi amor! Estoy bien. Enseguida voy para allá", "Se fue con su **churri** al cine, vuelven pronto".

Variations: Pichurri.

Ciego

Definition: Drunk or high.

Origin: Its origin is uncertain but it can be understood that when someone is drunk he (or she) doesn't know very well what he is doing, he can even lose consciousness, which could be similar to blindness in the sense that after being drunk many times one doesn't know what one did.

Use: There are many ways to use this word, for example "Estar", "Ponerse", "Ir ciego".

Examples: "**Me he puesto tan ciego** que no recuerdo nada".

Variations: Estar ciego, ponerse ciego, andar ciego, ir ciego.

Cojones

Definition: Balls, testicles.

Origin: It comes from the Latin coleo, 'leather bag'.

Use: The word 'cojones' is used to express various moods, usually anger. Similar to 'fuck' or 'hell'.

Examples: "¿Qué **cojones** es esto?".

Variations: Conjoncillo, cojoncito, cojonazo, cojoncete.

Cojonudo

Definition: Very good, excellent, unbeatable.

Origin: It comes from the word 'cojones' (balls).

Use: It's used to describe something that is great or to agree positively.

Examples: "Aquel coche era **cojonudo**. No había otro mejor". "¡**Cojonudo**!. Nos vemos mañana en la playa".

Variations: N/A.

Colega

Definition: Companion, friend, person with whom you get along or for whom you feel sympathy.

Origin: The literal translation to English is 'colleague'. It comes from the Latin collega 'companion of magistracy' and, by extension, 'person who performs the same function as another'.

Use: In colloquial language it's used to refer to a friend.

Examples: "Vamos con unos **colegas** a tomar unas cervezas más tarde".

Variations: Coleguita, coleguilla, colegui, colegazo.

Compi

Definition: Flatmate, roommate.

Origin: The word 'compi' comes from the abbreviation of 'compañero', which means 'partner'. The term 'compañero' etymologically comes from the Latin 'cumpanis' (cum: with panis: bread), whose literal translation is 'with bread' giving it the meaning of 'sharing the bread' or 'those who share the bread', 'eat of the same bread'.

Use: Usually used to refer to a flatmate, for example: "Su compi de piso también viene a la fiesta", which translates to: "Her/his flatmate also comes to the party."

Examples: "Mi **compi** toca muy bien la guitarra".

Variations: Compañero.

Coña

Definition: Joke, humor.

Origin: It comes from the word 'coño' (vagina).

Use: Used to say that something is a joke. You can say 'Es coña' or 'Estás de coña'.

Examples: "¿Qué te ha tocado la lotería? ¡Venga ya! Estás de **coña**, ¿no?".

Variations: Coñita, ni de coña.

Coñazo

Definition: Something or someone very boring or irritating.

Origin: It comes from the word coño (vagina), adding the suffix -azo to emphasize.

Use: Used to say that something or someone

is boring or unbearable. It can be used saying "Algo es un coñazo" or "Un coñazo de...".

Examples: "Vaya **coñazo** de película".

Variations: N/A.

Cotilla

Definition: Gossipy.

Origin: The origin of the term comes from a woman named María de la Trinidad, who lived in Spain during the reign of Fernando VII, and also known by the nickname Tía Cotilla. Although there is no agreement on the origin of this nickname, it's thought that it could be due to her last name or the use of a type of bra that the women of the time used and that received the name of gossip.

This woman was a political fanatic, led a gang of criminals, and was involved in several murders committed in 1835. According to historians, Aunt Cotilla had a strong character, a very rude vocabulary, and quite antisocial behavior.

Use: You can say 'cotilla' (gossipy), 'cotillear' (to gossip) or 'cotilleo' (act of gossiping).

Examples: "Esa tía siempre está **cotilleando** en voz alta".

Variations: Cotillear (to gossip), cotilleo (gossip).

Crack

Definition: Person who excels at something.

Origin: The origin of this word is uncertain. According to French sources it seems that the term comes from the world of horse riding. The horses that finished first were usually called 'crack', since in English 'to crack' meant 'to brag'.

Use: Used to praise someone who is very good at something.

Examples: "Mi primo es un **crack** en los videojuegos".

Variations: N/A.

Cubata

Definition: Cocktail.

Origin: Chronicles tell that the 'cubata' was born in Cuba during the War of Independence (1895-1898). The victorious Cubans celebrated their Hispanic independence with the cry of "Viva Cuba Libre", toasted with rum and arms raised.

On a very hot day, the US soldiers were in a bar in Old Havana, celebrating, laughing and sweating, when Colonel Russell ordered a refreshing drink to be prepared. The skillful Havana waiter then combined rum with Coca-Cola and ice, and the colonel, delighted with the invention, gave it to his troops to try. Instantly the soldiers asked for a round and the "toast" was made in Spanish exclaiming '¡Viva Cuba Libre!' (Long live free Cuba!), Baptizing the famous cocktail.

Use: Although its origin refers to the cocktail that is known as 'Cuba Libre', other cocktails can also be called 'cubata'.

Examples: "Aquella noche nos tomamos tantos **cubatas** que acabamos borrachísimos".

Variations: N/A.

Currar

Definition: To work, to make an effort.

Origin: It comes from the Caló language.

Use: It's used to refer to the act of working or to say that something has taken a lot of effort.

Examples: "Hoy he **currado** hasta las 8pm. ¡Estoy muerto!", "¡Qué guapo!. ¡Te lo has currado bien eh!".

Variations: Curro.

Cutre

Definition: Something of poor quality, very bad, poorly preserved, that doesn't receive care or attention.

Origin: Some experts consider that its origin may be linked to the French word "Croute", which was used in the 19th century as an adjective in the world of painting, to identify a bad artist, with little effort and less results.

Use: The word 'cutre' can also be used to describe a petty, wicked, mean act. It's also related to the lack of manners, norms and rules of etiquette, as well as inappropriate social behaviors such as taking off shoes in the subway, which for many would be somewhat 'cutre'.

Examples: "Qué coche tan **cutre**, ni siquiera tiene aire acondicionado".

Variations: Cutrón, cutrillo, cutrazo.

Dar caña

Definition: To speed it up. To hurry up.

Origin: In the past, whips or rods made from

the branches of the plant known as 'cañaheja' were used. These branches were used to whip cattle or horses to speed up the pace or not get out of the way, but they were also used by some people when they wanted to inflict physical punishment on someone (either to whip them on the back, buttocks or palm).

Use: The expression 'dar caña' (also in the form 'meter caña') is used to colloquially refer to the act of recriminating or provoking someone to do something, hurry up or finish it. These expressions are also used to refer to the fact of giving/putting intensity or speed ("¡métele caña al coche!", "¡dale caña!"). So it can be used in any informal conversation to tell someone to hurry up or speed up a vehicle.

Examples: "**Dale caña** tío, ya se está haciendo tarde", "¡**Dale caña**! La luz ya cambió a verde".

Variations: N/A.

De lujo

Definition: Great, very good.

Origin: The literal translation to English is 'of luxury'. Luxury symbolizes perfection and excellence, so it can be understood that something luxurious is something perfect.

Use: It can be used in any informal context instead of 'perfect' or 'great'.

Examples: "Esa blusa nueva te queda **de lujo**", "Este vino me sienta **de lujo**".

Variations: N/A.

De puta madre

Definition: Excellent, very good.

Origin: It literally translates to 'of bitch mother', but the meaning is very different.
By combining words as different as "mother" and "bitch" most believe that the meaning is an insult, which exists and would be "Tu puta madre". However, the meaning is the opposite when you say 'de puta madre', probably to give a little sarcasm.

Use: It should only be used with trusted people

as it's a rather vulgar expression. Spanish people use "de puta madre" to say that something is very good.

Examples: "La fiesta estuvo de **puta madre**". "La película es de **puta madre**".

Variations: N/A.

Echar la bronca

Definition: To discuss, to have an altercation.

Origin: The literal translation to English is 'to throw the fight'. According to the DRAE 'bronca' comes from the Latin *bruncus*, a word that comes from the combination of *broccus* and *truncus* meaning 'sharp stick'. Maybe that's why the word 'broncos' is referred to untamed horses.

Use: Used to indicate that someone has started or is about to start an argument.

Examples: "María me **echó la bronca** por la música alta otra vez".

Variations: N/A.

Encabronarse

Definition: To get mad, to get pissed off.

Origin: The word 'encabronarse' comes from the word 'cabrón' (refer to that word for the origin). It refers to the act of getting mad.

Use: It should only be used with trusted people as it is too vulgar a word.

Examples: "Me **encabroné** cuando vi la multa en mi coche".

Variations: Encabronado.

Es una pasada

Definition: Immoderate, excessive or very good action.

Origin: It literally means 'it's a passed'. The origin of this expression is uncertain, although we can understand from the word 'pasada' that the action has passed the limits of the normal.

Use: It's used when something seems very good to us. You could also say: "¡Es un pasote!" o "¡Es un flipe!", even more colloquial expressions.

Examples: "Esa jugada **ha sido una pasada**".

Variations: Es un pasote.

Espabilado

Definition: Smart, savvy.

Origin: In its origin the term began to be used as 'despabilar' and we find its origin in the union of the prefix 'des' (negation, deprivation, outside of) and 'pabilo' (wick that is in wax candles and formerly in oil lamps or lamps). Despabilar (and later espabilar) was the act of removing the already burned part of the wick and with this the flame was intensified, giving more and better light.

Hence, the term began to be used as a synonym

for the action of inciting or stimulating someone to make them perform more or indicate how awake and resourceful they are.

Use: A person is said to be 'espabilado' (or despabilado) as a clear reference to how intelligent and awake he/she is in any situation in life, and there are many occasions when the term (and its multiple variants) is also used as an interjection to tell someone to wake up (either because they are asleep or because they do not know something).

Examples: "Este niño es muy **espabilado** para su edad", "¡**Espabila**, que vamos a llegar tarde!".

Variations: Despabilado.

Estar hasta la polla

Definition: Being tired or bored of something.

Origin: The literal translation is 'to be until the dick'. As we already know, the word 'polla' can be used for positive and negative things, in this case is a negative thing.

Use: Use it when you are tired of something. It's a vulgar term so it should only be used with people you know.

Examples: "Estoy **hasta la polla** de tus quejas".

Variations: Tener hasta la polla.

Farra

Definition: Party, group fun.

Origin: The word 'farra' possibly comes from the Portuguese farra, and this perhaps from the Arabic dialect ferḥa, party.

Use: Usually said 'Irse de farra'.

Examples: "Se fueron **de farra** al puerto".

Variations: Andar de farra.

Finde

Definition: Weekend.

Origin: Short for 'fin de semana'.

Use: Its use is simple, it serves to replace 'fin de semana' word that can be very long in informal conversations.

Examples: "Qué planes tienes para el **finde**?".

Variations: N/A.

Flipar

Definition: To get impressed by something.

Origin: Its origin is found in the English verb 'to flip'. Hence the idea of turning your mind 'Flip your mind'.

Use: Used when something surprises you a lot.

Examples: "**Flipo** con los nuevos drones, parecen muy divertidos".

Variations: Flipado, flipao, flipante.

Friki

Definition: It's a colloquial term to refer to a person whose hobbies, behavior or clothing are unusual.

Origin: It comes from the English word freaky, although its literal translation would be 'geek'.

Use: It can be used to describe or insult. You can say: 'Es un friki' (He's a geek) or 'Es un friki de' (He's a geek of).

Examples: "Es un **friki** de los juegos de mesa, mira la colección que tiene".

Variations: Friqui.

Gilipollas

Definition: Stupid, silly.

Origin: Its origin dates back to 16th century Madrid, when Mr. Baltasar Gil Imón, a Prosecutor from the Council of the Treasury, attended parties and events with his two daughters, a little ugly and not too smart. When people saw them, they whispered sarcastically: "There goes Mr. Gil with his pollas (girls) again", deriving in the term "gilipollas".

Use: It should only be used with close friends or to insult people (if you want problems).

Examples: "Ese tío es un **gilipollas**, echando la basura en la calle".

Variations: N/A.

Gilipollez

Definition: Very stupid, absurd or irrelevant thing or action.

Origin: It comes from the word 'gilipollas'.

Use: It's used to describe something silly or irrelevant, 'Es una gilipollez' (It's bullshit) or 'Déjate de gilipolleces' (Stop doing bullshit).

Examples: "No me vengas con **gilipolleces** y ponte a currar".

Variations: N/A.

Guarro

Definition: Which is either very dirty or sloppy.

Origin: Formed in the language from the onomatopoeia 'Guarr', which imitates the sound of an animal.

Use: You can say 'Es muy guarro' or 'Es un(a) guarro(a)'.

Examples: "Eres un **guarro**, siempre dejas comida del día anterior en la mesa".

Variations: Guarrada.

Guay

Definition: Which is very good or extraordinary.

Origin: From the Gothic wái (onomatopoeic voice), that holds the same meaning.

Use: Used to show surprise or to show approval for something.

Examples: "¡Qué **guay**! Dónde lo compraste?" "… **guay**, entonces a qué hora vamos al cine?".

Variations: N/A.

Hostia

Definition: Strong blow. It can be accidental or intentional. It can also mean a sort of exclamation indicating surprise.

Origin: From the Latin hostia, "offering, sacrificial victim", from hostire, "to strike".

Use: It's used to speak of a strong blow 'Se dio una hostia'. It can also be used to express surprise 'Hostia, no lo puedo creer'. It's a rather vulgar word so it should only be used with close friends.

Examples: "¡Joder, tío! ¡Vaya **hostia** que me acabo de dar contra la mesa!", "¡**Hostia**! ¿Qué le pasó a tu coche?".

Variations: Hostión, hostiazo, hostia puta.

Irse la olla

Definition: Go crazy, do crazy things.

Origin: 'Irse la olla' literally means 'to go the pot', and it has a very interesting story.

The origin of this expression takes us back to France in the mid-18th century, specifically to 1739, when Louise Isabella of France, daughter of Louis XV, prepared her farewell party for the French court to go to Spain to live with her husband, Prince Philip, son of Philip V. The cook chosen for the occasion was Jean-Luc Sagnol, who had made his name in Marseilles in previous years.

It is said that Sagnol promised Louis XV the best oyster and lobster soup that a French monarch had ever tasted. On the day of the ceremony, word had spread about the dish Sagnol was preparing and expectations were very high. When the time came for the first course, Sagnol announced the soup with a grandiloquent speech, where he exalted all the virtues of a recipe he had worked on for fourteen years.

Afterwards, there was an event that no one has ever been able to explain. When Sagnol returned to the kitchen to put the soup on the plates, the pot in which it was found had disappeared. It seems that this was some kind of plot by the kitchen helpers, who Sagnol had treated with special harshness in those days, but the truth is that it could never be proved and that the pot never appeared, not even empty.

With his career completely ruined by this fact, Sagnol went into a state of mental derangement, came out to the hall and approached the king and said laughingly, "Majestad, se me ha ido la olla" (Your Majesty, my pot is gone). Louis XV, feeling deceived and mocked by the laughter of the cook, got into a rage and had him arrested. While the guards were taking him out of the Sagnol palace, he kept shouting in a hysterical way "¡Se me ha ido la olla! ¡Se me ha ido la olla!". The story quickly spread throughout France and since then the expression "irse la olla" has been associated with people who have gone mad or who do things without meaning.

Use: Used to say that someone has gone crazy. You can say both: 'Se le fue la olla' and 'se le ha ido la olla'.

Examples: "¿Qué hace este tío?. No sé, **se le ha ido la olla**".

Variations: Irse la pinza.

Joder

Definition: Expression of anger or surprise.

Origin: It comes from the Latin 'futuere' which means to copulate, although it's rarely used to describe that action.

Use: Used to show anger or surprise at someone or something.

Examples: "¡**Joder**, qué bien! ¿No?", "¡No me molestes más, joder!".

Variations: Jolín.

Jodido

Definition: A very difficult thing or situation.

Origin: It comes from the word 'joder', which as we know means 'to fuck'. It can be understood that something or someone 'jodido' is someone that has been 'fucked' by the situation it is facing.

Use: This word is used to say that something is very difficult or that you are in a difficult situation yourself.

Examples: "Tengo el hombro **jodido**, tengo que hacer rehabilitación".

Variations: Jodidísimo, jodidazo.

Liarse

Definition: It's a word that has many meanings, one of the most used by younger people is to kiss or maintain a love relationship. The second meaning can refer to being very busy or in trouble.

Origin: The word "liar" (to make a tangle) comes from the Latin ligare (to tie). For this reason, 'liarse' can be associated with getting entangled, either in a problem or in a love relationship.

Use: You can either say 'Liarse' (reflexive) or 'Estar liado'.

Examples: "Finalmente **os liasteis** o todo quedó ahí", "Ahora estoy muy **liado**, llámame más tarde".

Variations: N/A.

Lío

Definition: Problem, mess.

Origin: The word 'lío' comes from 'liar' and this one comes from the Latin ligare (to tie). For this reason a problematic or confusing situation is called a 'lío'.

Use: It can be used as a synonym for the word problem/trouble.

Examples: "Esto de la política es un **lío**", "¡Qué **lío** en el que te has metido!".

Variations: N/A.

Macho

Definition: A word used to refer to a person of the male sex or simply to express surprise or anger.

Origin: The literal translation is 'male'. It's not clear why it's used to express surprise or anger.

Use: You can say: '¡Macho! ¿Qué pasó?' (Man, what happened!) or '¡Joder, macho!' (Dammit, man!). Whoever says it or to whom it refers does not necessarily have to be male.

Examples: "¡Joder, **macho**! ¿Siempre tienes que usar mis cosas o qué?".

Variations: N/A.

Madre mía

Definition: Expression that is used to show exclamation towards something that very surprising.

Origin: The origin of this expression is unknown, but it's probably related to the fact that when we were children and got surprised by something, we used to call our mothers to share it with them, whether it was something good or bad.

Use: It can be used for both positive and negative situations.

Examples: "¡**Madre mía**, tú sí que tienes suerte eh!", "¡**Madre mía**, qué horrible te queda el peinado!".

Variations: N/A.

Majo

Definition: Good people. That by his appearance, behavior or sympathy makes others pleasant.

Origin: Its origin is uncertain. The most extended version gives it as a derivation of 'majar' (to hit).

Use: Used to refer to someone we like.

Examples: "El Carlos es muy **majo**, me ayudó sin pedírselo".

Variations: Majete.

Mala leche

Definition: The expression 'mala leche' is used to designate someone who shows bad character, bad temper or bad intentions.

Origin: Mala leche literally means 'bad milk'. The origin of the expression goes back to the ancient belief that the milk used for breastfeeding influenced character. For example, Aristotle claimed that there was a certain social organization that was determined by the milk that was sucked. Thus, the natural members of a village were those who had ingested the same milk. For his part, St. Augustine recommended that Christian children should not be breastfed by pagan mothers, because this would negatively influence their faith. Doctors also advised that they should seek out physically and mentally healthy wet nurses.

Use: You can either say 'tener mala leche' or 'andar de mala leche'.

Examples: "Estoy de muy **mala leche**, me acaban de poner otra multa", "Esa tía anda de muy

mala leche".

Variations: Estar de mala leche, andar de mala leche, llevar mala leche.

Marrón

Definition: Indesirable and annoying task or thing that nobody wants.

Origin: Its exact origin is uncertain. One theory is that 'marrón' refers to the term that the French use to say "chestnut". And that a chestnut is synonymous in Spanish with a problem. Therefore, eating a chestnut or a 'marrón' was equivalent to eating a problem.

Use: It can be used as a substitute for the word problem, for example: "Vaya marrón lo de la multa que te pusieron". It can also be used in combination with the word 'eat', for example: "Si no resolvemos esto nos vamos a comer un marrón" ('If we do not solve it now we are going to eat a brown when it is more serious).

Examples: "¡El marrón que te vas a comer si no bajas de ahí!".

Variations: Marronazo, marronaco, marron-cillo, marroncito, marroncete.

Matao

Definition: Loser.

Origin: The correct word would be 'matado', which translated to English would be 'killed' but many times the 'd' is omitted. It can be understood that a 'matao' is someone who has sacrificed (matado) himself to get something and finally has not achieved it.

Use: Used as an insult to someone who is considered a failure.

Examples: "Llevas cinco años tocando la guitarra y sigues siendo un **matao**".

Variations: Matado.

Me la suda

Definition: Being indifferent to something.

Origin: The full expression actually is 'Me suda la polla' (My dick sweats). As it's well known, something that sweats (it secretes sweat or a liquid through its pores) slips and there is nothing more 'slippery' than indifference towards a subject, but if we add to the expression (and with the purpose of emphasizing the answer) the male sexual member we manage to highlight the degree of disinterest towards the subject.

Use: You can say 'Me la suda' o ' Me suda la polla algo'. You have to be careful in the second case since it's very vulgar to say it.

Examples: "A mí **me la suda**, voy a la fiesta de todas formas", "**Me sudan la polla** tus historias".

Variations: Me suda la polla.

Mogollón

Definition: Very abundant quantity of something.

Origin: From the Italian moccobello or the Catalan mogobells (tip) and those of the Arab مقابل (muqābil , "compensation"). It's uncertain how its meaning changed to refer to something very abundant.

Use: It can be used alone: "Te quiero mogollón". It can also be used followed by 'de': "Mogollón de perros".

Examples: "Había **mogollón** de gente".

Variations: Mogollonazo, mogolloncete.

Molar

Definition: To like something very much.

Origin: It comes from the Caló language.

Use: It can be used as a reflexive ver, like in 'me mola algo' or as a non-reflexive verb like in 'eso mola mucho'.

Examples: "Me **mola** mucho tu nueva mochila", "El nuevo museo **mola** mucho, tiene de todo".

Variations: Molón/molona.

Montar

Definition: To organize, to assemble.

Origin: It comes from the vulgar Latin, montare which means 'to climb a mountain'.

Use: Among its various meanings it can be used instead of the word 'organizing', for example: "Voy a montar una despedida de soltero" (I'm going to organize a bachelor party). It can also be used instead of 'assemble/build', for example: "He montado el mueble yo solo" (I've built the sofa on my own).

Examples: "Vamos a **montar** una fiesta cuando te vayas", "Habéis **montado** un chiringuito aquí!".

Variations: N/A.

Movida

Definition: Confusing or unclear situation that is generally negative or conflictive.

Origin: It comes from the verb 'mover' (to move), and it's still uncertain how it acquired that meaning.

Use: It's used when we want to refer to anything, generally a negative situation. It can be perfectly replaced by the word 'asunto' (matter/issue), for example: "Esa movida la quiero resolver yo solo" (I want to solve that issue by myself).

Examples: "Al asociarse con los traficantes se metió en una **movida** que le arruinó".

Variations: N/A.

No pasa nada

Definition: There's no problem. All good.

Origin: It literally translates to 'Nothing happens'.

Use: It's used to say that there's no problem and things will be alright.

Examples: "Perdón, ¿Te pisé muy fuerte?. **No pasa nada**. está bien".

Variations: N/A.

Ostras

Definition: Euphemism for the exclamation of surprise '¡Hostia!' (Damn!).

Origin: The literal translation in English is 'Oysters'. Like all euphemism, the word 'ostras'' sounds very much like 'hostia', so it began to be used as a substitute in less vulgar situations.

Use: It can be used in the same way as the word 'hostia' although it sounds less offensive.

Examples: "**Ostras,** dejé la llave en la puerta".

Variations: N/A.

Papeleo

Definition: Bureaucratic procedure, paperwork.

Origin: The literal translation to English would be 'papering'. It comes from the word 'papel' (paper), and is usually the material on which all bureaucratic procedures have to be formalized.

Use: The most appropriate word would be 'trámite' (paperwork) but 'papeleo' can also be used in any formal or informal situation.

Examples: "Esto de ser autónomo es mucho **papeleo**".

Variations: N/A.

Pasta

Definition: Money.

Origin: The literal translation for 'pasta' is dough or paste, and the reason why money is called like this is because in the past, there was a difference between money itself (coins) and 'pasta' (the uncoined metal). The reason why is that when the raw metal was melted it had a dough-like appearance, and once cold it lost that appearance but kept the same name.

Use: It can be perfectly replaced by the word money, for example: "Ya no me queda pasta para comprar más cerveza", which means "I have no more money to buy more beer".

Examples: "Ese bolso cuesta una **pasta,** conozco una tienda más barata".

Variations: Pastón, pastizal, pastucia, pastanaga, pastita, pastilla.

Pavo(a)

Definition: Individual, person (slightly pejorative).

Origin: The word 'pavo' literally means turkey. It's uncertain why an uneducated person is called a 'pavo', but it may be because the turkey, like most birds, is not very smart.

Use: It can be used to replace the word 'tonto' (fool) or 'tío' (dude). It's not necessarily used to insult.

Examples: "Los **pavos** del otro equipo piensan que nos pueden ganar".

Variations: Pavorro.

Pavos

Definition: Euros, dollars.

Origin: The word 'euros/dollars' started to be called as 'pavos' in the year 1930, approximately. 5 pesetas (former Spanish currency) were called a 'pavo' (turkey), because it is exactly what this animal was worth. In America, dollars are also called "bucks" (deer), because in the 1700s the skin of these animals was used as a medium of exchange for other things of value, as a substitute for money. So, a Spanish dubbing director decided to use "pavos" as the equivalent of "bucks" in his films, and it's still used today.

Use: It can be used to replace the word 'euros' or 'dollars'.

Examples: "Préstame 20 **pavos** que me quedé sin pasta".

Variations: Pavorro.

Peña

Definition: Group of people, specially when they share something in common.

Origin: The literal translation to English is 'Big rock', but the exact origin of it's meaning in this case is very uncertain. The word peña can refer, among other things, to a group of individuals who come together to carry out certain activities. By extension, the term also refers to the meeting itself and the place where the meeting takes place.

Use: It can be used to refer to a particular group of people or any group of people.

Examples: "Saldrás hoy con tu **peña?**", "La **peña** está loca, por qué aplauden ahora?".

Variations: N/A.

Petado

Definition: Full.

Origin: From Catalan petar (to explode). It's not clear how the word 'petar' came to mean full but perhaps it means that a place is so full that it has exploded, figuratively speaking.

Use: It's generally used with places.

Examples: "La sala del cine estaba **petada,** no entraba ni una persona".

Variations: Petao.

Petar

Definition: To explode, to burst.

Origin: From Catalan petar, which means 'strong noise done by something that crashed or exploited in a violent way.

Use: It can be perfectly replaced by the word 'explode', for example: "He comido tanto que voy a petar", which means "I've eaten so much that I'm going to explode".

Examples: "El estrés me mata, estoy por **petar** en cualquier momento".

Variations: N/A.

Pica-pica

Definition: Food that consists of varied meals that are presented in small portions and that is taken at will without an established order.

Origin: The word pica-pica literally means 'bite-bite', and it refers to the act of eating in small bites (snacks).

Use: Usually offered to attendees of an event.

Examples: "Ofrecieron a los asistentes un **pica-pica** y una copa de champán".

Variations: N/A.

Pijo

Definition: Term used to describe high social position, generally attributed to young people who follow the latest fashion and has very characteristic manners and way of speaking.

Origin: The literal translation to english would be 'posh'. It's origin is uncertain, perhaps it comes from pija, from the old Castilian pixa that refers to the pennis.

Use: It can be used for men and women, 'pijo' and 'pija', generally derogatory.

Examples: "Ese es un bar **pijo,** mejor vamos al de la esquina que es más barato".

Variations: Pijillo, pijito, pijín, pijazo.

Pillar

Definition: Enter into possession of something (buying it, stealing it or in any way).

Origin: The word 'pillar' comes from the Italian pigliare (to catch) and this seems to come from the Latin pileare (to steal, loot).

Use: It can be used in the same way as 'catch' or 'take'.

Examples: "**Pilla** un par de cervezas en el supermercado de la esquina".

Variations: N/A.

Pirarse

Definition: Leaving a place.

Origin: From the Caló language. It comes from the word 'pira' which means 'escape'.

Use: It's a reflexive verb that is used to say that someone or oneself is leaving or already left a place.

Examples: "Marta se **piró** temprano de la fiesta, tenía que trabajar temprano".

Variations: N/A.

Ponerse al día

Definition: Expression used among friends or acquaintances to meet and learn about each other's news. Usually when they haven't seen each other for a long time.

Origin: The literal translation to English is 'to put to day' and it has the same meaning as 'to catch-up'. The 'al día' part shows the need for knowing the latest news until the day of the catch-up.

Use: Generally used among friends who haven't seen each other for a long time or who have a lot to tell.

Examples: "¿Te parece si nos tomamos un café y **nos ponemos al día**?".

Variations: N/A.

Pringado

Definition: A person that's easily fooled. Loser.

Origin: It comes from 'pringar' which means to soak, wet or moisten with 'pringue' (fat) bread or any food.
Back in the days the 'pringado' was one that was marked by 'pringue' dictated by the judge. The one who committed a misdemeanor received a trickle of oil or hot butter on his skin so that he would be marked for life, so that it would be 'noted' that he had a record when he was arrested again wherever he was.

Use: You can say 'Eres un pringado' or 'Qué pringado'. It's normally used to mock friends or other people that have been fooled.

Examples: "Eres un **pringado** tío, ya deja de pensar en ella".

Variations: Pringao, pringadillo, pringadete, pringueras, pringui.

Puta(o)

Definition: Intensifier of a noun or adjective, usually with a negative meaning.

Origin: Its original meaning is 'prostitute', it comes from the Latin putta (girl, especially "street girl").

Use: It's used to intensify a noun like '¡puto coronavirus!' (fucking coronavirus!). Generally used in a negative sense.

Examples: "¡Este **puto** móvil nunca funciona bien!".

Variations: N/A.

Putada

Definition: Unpleasant situation without remedy.

Origin: It comes from the word 'puta' that means prostitute. Since the word 'puta' is associated with something negative 'putada' is also linked in the same way, in this case to describe an unpleasant situation.

Use: Use with unpleasant or even unfair situations.

Examples: "Vaya **putada,** ¿Te pusieron una multa otra vez?".

Variations: Putadón, putadita, putadilla, putadica.

¡Qué dices!

Definition: It's used to describe surprises and disbelief.

Origin: It literally means '¡What do you say!'. Perhaps it appeared because when we hear something too surprising we need it to be repeated in order to believe it.

Use: It can be used in any informal context and can be complemented with '¡Qué fuerte!', when you want to express even more surprise.

Examples: "¡**Qué dices**! ¡No lo puedo creer!".

Variations: N/A.

¡Qué fuerte!

Definition: Colloquially used to describe something that surprises a lot.

Origin: It literally translates to 'How strong!' in English. The exact origin of the expression is not clear, but it could come from 'fuerte sorpresa' (strong surprise).

Use: Generally used when we are surprised by something that just happened.

Examples: "**Qué fuerte** lo que me has dicho!".

Variations: N/A.

¡Qué máquina!

Definition: Expression of praise for someone who performs very well at something.

Origin: Translated to English would be 'What a machine!'. The word 'máquina' is used to describe the flawless performance of a task, such as machines do, most of the time.

Use: Used to praise someone who does a very good job in any field.

Examples: "¿Has visto cómo juega al tenis? **¡Que máquina!**".

Variations: N/A.

Que no veas

Definition: Big, important. Intensifying phrase of what has just been said.

Origin: The literal translation is 'that you don't see'. It's not clear how this expression originated but it can mean that it's something so surprising that you will not even see it, although it can also be something so surprising that it is better that you do not see it.

Use: Generally used when we are surprised by something that just happened or something big.

Examples: "Hace un calor **que no veas**".

Variations: N/A.

Que te cagas

Definition: Like the phrase 'Que no veas'. This is an intensifying phrase, although more vulgar.

Origin: The literal translation is 'that you shit yourself'. 'Cagar' means to defecate and comes from the Latin cacare, and this from the proto-Indo-European * kakka-, "excrement".

Use: It's used in the same way as 'que no veas' although it's a little more vulgar because it says 'cagas' (shit), so you should only use it with close friends only.

Examples: "Hace un frío **que te cagas**".

Variations: N/A.

¡Qué va!

Definition: Expression that serves to show surprise and disbelief.

Origin: The literal translation is 'what goes', and it means something like 'no way!' in English. Its origin is uncertain but it could come from the phrase 'que va a saber' (what he/her is going to know) or 'que va a ser' (what it's going to be), that also express surprise and disbelief towards a certain situation.

Use: It's used in response to a statement that is considered unlikely or disagreed with. For example: "¿Te molesta que te llamen tonto?. ¡Qué va! Me da risa" ("Does it bother you to be called a fool?. No way! It makes me laugh").

Examples: "¿Ya estas cansado? ¡**Qué va**, puedo correr mucho más!".

Variations: N/A.

Quedada

Definition: Meeting with friends or acquaintances to develop a common activity.

Origin: It comes from the word 'quedar' (to stay).

Use: It's used as a noun, so you can replace it the word 'reunión' (meeting), for example: "Siempre organizan quedadas (reuniones) los sábados" (They always organize meetups on Saturdays).

Examples: "Voy a una **quedada** con unos amigos de la natación el sábado, ¿Te vienes?".

Variations: Quedar.

Rayarse

Definition: Losing patience or mind for some reason; lose one's head.

Origin: The literal translation of 'rayar' is 'to scratch'. The origin is in the analogy of the 'loco con el disco rayado' (crazy man with the scratched disc). When the disc is scratched it makes the stylus (niddle) jump from one side to the other, resulting in inconsistent sounds. Hence, when someone gets 'rayado' (scratched) it is because they are going crazy about something, figuratively speaking.

Use: It's a reflexive verb so it must always be accompanied by a reflexive pronoun, for example: 'No te rayes' or 'Me estoy rayando'.

Examples: "Deja de **rayarte** con eso y tómate un descanso".

Variations: Rayado, rayao.

Salir de los huevos

Definition: To do something for no reason other than because you feel like it.

Origin: It literally means 'to come out of the eggs'. The word 'huevos' (eggs) colloquially refers to testicles. The testicles are a symbol of testosterone and virility, therefore this phrase alludes to a dominant male attitude of someone that does what he/she wants regardless of what others think.

Use: It's used to express firmness and indifference to the consequences that acts may have, for example: "En esta casa hago lo que me sale de los huevos" (In this house I do what I want).

Examples: "Al parecer lo hizo porque le **salió de los huevos**, pero luego verá las consecuencias".

Variations: N/A.

Sentar bien/ mal algo

Definition: To please or annoy one thing.

Origin: 'Sentar' literally means 'to sit', so 'sentar bien' means 'to sit well with'.

Use: It's a reflexive verb, therefore it should be used with a reflexive pronoun, for example: "Esa hamburguesa no te va a sentar bien, es muy tarde" (That burger's not gonna sit well with you, it's too late). We shouldn't confuse it with 'sentarse bien' which means 'to sit (down) properly'.

Examples: "La meditación por las mañanas **me sienta muy bien**, comienzo mejor el día".

Variations: N/A.

Ser la hostia

Definition: To be something very important.

Origin: From the Latin hostia, "offering, sacrificial victim". Hostia is a curse word that's used broadly in Spanish language, depending on the context it can refer to something positive or negative.

Use: It's a rather vulgar word so it should be used with close friends, even though it has a positive meaning. It can be intensified with the word 'puta" before or after, for example: "Joder tío, eres la puta hostia en el fútbol".

Examples: "Ella **es la hostia**, habla 4 idiomas y solo tiene 15 años".

Variations: Ser la leche.

Tener buena/ mala pinta

Definition: Good or bad external appearance of something.

Origin: In the past 'Pinta' was the name used to designate the sign that the cards of the Spanish deck have on their ends and that, without having to fully discover them, one can know which suit the card is (Clubs, Diamonds, Hearts, Spades) and, therefore, to know by the 'Pinta' if you have a good or bad hand.

It was frequent to hear among the players such typical phrases as: "A ver qué pinta tienen las cartas que me has dado" (Let's see what the cards you have given me look like) and/or think to themselves "Estas cartas no tienen muy buena pinta" (These cards do not look very good).

Over time this expression became popular in everyday language and began to be used to define many people by their clothing (good or bad 'pinta') and also to judge situations or places by their appearance: "Hoy tiene pinta de que va a llover" (Today it looks like it is going to rain), "Según sea la pinta del restaurante nos quedamos a comer o no" (Depending on how the restaurant looks, we stay for lunch or not).

Use: It can be used alone or before the word good/bad, for example: "Qué pinta tiene el restaurante al que vamos a cenar?" (How does the restaurant where we are having dinner look like?) or "Eso no tiene buena pinta, mejor no lo comas" (That doesn't look good, don't eat it).

Examples: "Estos tomates **tienen muy mala pinta**, no los voy a comer".

Variations: N/A.

Tío

Definition: A generic term for calling another person, especially if you have trust or friendship with them.

Origin: 'Tío' literally means uncle. It's uncertain why it's used to designate someone that is not related to us, but maybe it's meant to create familiarity. This also happens in other Spanish speaking countries where words like 'compadre', 'cuñado' or 'hermano' are also used with the same intention.

Use: It's perhaps one of the most used words in the Spanish colloquial language. It's used as a substitute for 'boy' or 'dude', for example: "Esa tía nunca me contesta las llamadas, siempre anda ocupada" or "¡Tío, ven aquí!".

Examples: "**Tío**, vamos a tomar una cerveza al bar de la esquina".

Variations: N/A.

Total

Definition: Word used to affirm with emphasis what has been said.

Origin: It's not known exactly why this word is used to express approval but it may come from the longer expression 'totalmente de acuerdo' which means 'fully agree'.

Use: Used to affirm with emphasis what has just been said.

Examples: "¿Has visto cómo me habló? ¡**Total**, es una grosera!".

Variations: N/A.

Tranqui

Definition: Calm state of mind.

Origin: 'Tranqui' is the abbreviation of "tranquilo".
The literal translation of tranquilo is 'calm'. It comes from the Latin tranquillus (beyond calm), composed with: The prefix trans- (beyond) and the root quiescere (calm down, rest).

Use: It can be used to describe a state of mind, a person or an issue, for example "Estoy muy tranqui, nadar me ayudó a relajarme" (I'm very calm, swimming helped me relax), "Ella es muy tranqui, todo se lo toma con calma" (She is very calm, she takes everything easy) or "Fue un finde tranqui, fui a leer al parque" (It was a chill weekend, I went to read in the park).

Examples: "Tranqui, no te enfades conmigo".

Variations: N/A.

Un duro

Definition: No money.

Origin: Word for 5 pesetas, former Spanish currency.

Use: Generally used to describe situations where you don't have enough money to do something.

Examples: "Tengo que encontrar trabajo cuanto antes, estoy sin **un duro**".

Variations: N/A.

Un huevo

Definition: A lot.

Origin: 'Huevo' means 'egg'. It's not known exactly why it's used for this purpose although knowing that 'huevo' in Spanish slang means 'testicle', you can understand that something that costs 'un huevo' (one testicle) is something very expensive (for a man) since there are only two.

Use: You can either say 'un huevo' or 'un huevo de'.

Examples: "Tiene **un huevo de** zapatos en el armario".

Variations: N/A.

¡Venga!

Definition: Expression used to show excitement or approval, similar to 'Let's go!' or 'Alright!'.

Origin: Its literal translation is 'Come' or 'It comes'. Its origin is uncertain but it might come from the expression "venga otro trago" (come another drink), widely used by customer in bars, as some articles have stated.

Use: It can be used to express excitement about something we want to start.

Examples: "¡**Venga,** que se hace tarde!".

Variations: N/A.

¡Y tanto!

Definition: Expression used to indicate approval.

Origin: The literal translation to English would be 'And much!'. The exact origin of this expression is unknown, but it might come from the longer expression '¡Y tanto más! (And so much more) which shows the strong will to do/accept something.

Use: It's generally used to express approval of something that has been previously requested.

Examples: "¿Puedo dejar mi sombrero en el perchero? ¡**Y tanto**! Déjame que yo lo pongo.".

Variations: N/A.

EL DILEMA DE MARTA

Characters

Marta

Marta is a 26-year-old girl from Galicia, where she lived with her parents until she was 24, when she decided to move to Barcelona to become independent and study a postgraduate degree in accounting.

Now Marta is an intern in a large accounting audit company, although she's actually passionate about sustainable development. She has a great sense of humor and is very friendly. At the same time she has insecurity issues that lead to occasional anxiety attacks and lack of sleep.

Raquel

Raquel is Marta's flatmate, she is 28 years old and comes from Madrid. Raquel has lived in Barcelona for 5 years and is a fairly independent girl who has lived away from home since she was 18 years old.

Raquel likes to help others overcome their fears. She feels special empathy for people with insecurity because that is how she felt when she left her family to live in other countries at a very young age.

Laura

Laura is Marta's boss. She is a very nervous and loud person, who does not get along with Marta and always leaves her extra work at the last minute.

Even though she appears to be nice on the outside, tends to be very manipulative, for example she told Marta many times that she would get hired by the company very soon just to keep her working as an intern.

Carlos

Carlos is Marta's roommate. He is 21 years old and is the typical posh boy who studies at a high society university in Barcelona. His parents support him and give him everything he wants.

Carlos likes to bring his soccer friends to the floor and almost always leaves everything messed up.

Luís

Luís is a friend of Marta's from meditation. He is Colombian and has been living in Barcelona for 4 years. He is passionate about the conservation of animals.

Introduction to the story

Marta is in a dilemma, on the one hand she wants to develop her professional career in her current company, she would like to be hired to earn more and allow herself a better quality of life since she currently shares an apartment with 4 more people, she has a very small room and makes barely enough to save a little. On the other hand, Marta is passionate about sustainable development, she watches many documentaries on this topic and would like to work on it one day. Luckily Marta is not alone, she has made good friends with her flatmate Raquel, who is also looking for something better in her life...

1. Laura es una borde

Marta regresa del trabajo a las 8 de la noche como es de costumbre últimamente. Es temporada alta en la empresa y tiene que trabajar hasta 10 horas diarias, a pesar de que aún sigue cobrando muy poco. Al regresar a casa Marta se encuentra en el ascensor con Raquel, su compañera de piso:

Raquel: ¡Qué pasa Marta! ¿Cómo ha ido el **curro**?

Marta: No soporto a la Laura, ¡Es una **borde**!

Raquel: ¿Con qué te salió esta vez? Siempre me cuentas cada cosa de ella, ¿Parece que está **chalada** la **tía** no?

Marta: Pues siempre está **cotilleando** en voz alta por teléfono, como si nadie le escuchara. Realmente **flipo** con ella. Además me da trabajo a última hora para que me quede hasta tarde en la oficina.

Raquel: ¿Pero por qué no **te piras** de esa empresa? Siempre regresas con historias, y además te explotan, ¡Mira a la hora que llegas!

Marta: No te olvides de la miseria que me pagan jaja. Creo que sería más feliz reciclando plástico.

Raquel: Para Marta, no digas **gilipolleces**.

Marta: Vale, vale. Oye, por cierto... ¿Sabes si Carlos está en casa? Le quería decir que no se olvide de limpiar el baño, que esta semana le tocaba a él.

Raquel: Pues estaba aquí más temprano pero se fue a jugar fútbol, parece que aún no ha limpiado.

Marta: ¡**Me cago en la leche**! ¡Este **chaval** se cree que puede hacer lo que quiera o qué!

Raquel: Bueno paciencia que ya limpiará. Te iba a preguntar, ¿Qué planes tienes para este **finde**?

Marta: Pues **tranqui**, quiero verme ese documental que te conté sobre el desarrollo sostenible. Estoy un poco nerviosa porque la próxima semana Laura me dice si me contratan o no, así que quiero tomarme el **finde** con calma. ¿Y tú?

Raquel: Sí recuerdo, siempre viene bien un **finde tranqui**. Pues yo estaré muy **liada**, estoy trabajando en un proyecto personal muy **chulo**, la próxima semana te cuento más detalles.

Marta: ¡Qué misteriosa! Vale, pues ya me contarás.

2. Un finde no muy tranqui

Marta quiere aprovechar el fin de semana para descansar, ha tenido una semana muy estresante en el trabajo así que quiere leer un poco, limpiar su habitación y ver un documental de desarrollo sostenible. El único problema es que Marta comparte piso con 4 personas más. Es la 1 de la mañana y Carlos, su compi de piso, ha decidido juntarse con sus amigos del fútbol en el salón, entonces Marta sale a hablar con él:

Marta: Oye Carlos, está bien que sea sábado pero, ¿No podéis piraros a otro lado? Ya es la 1 de la mañana y necesito dormir.

Carlos: Pero, ¿Por qué no te vienes con nosotros? ¡Hay **birra** y **pica-pica**!

Marta: No es **coña** Carlos, he tenido una semana muy **jodida** en el **curro** y lo único que necesito es dormir.

Carlos: Pero este piso lo compartimos todos, no sólo es tuyo. Además aún es la 1 a. m, hemos quedado en que los **findes** se puede hacer **botellón** hasta las 2 a. m, ¿no?

Marta: Pues sí, pero siempre te quedas más tiempo y dejas todo muy **guarro**.

Carlos: No es verdad, siempre limpio al día siguiente, ¡Para de **echarme la bronca** con eso!

Marta: Mira, dejémoslo así. ¿Podrías bajarle un poco a la música?

Carlos: Vale, le bajo.

3. Los cabrones de recursos humanos

El lunes por la mañana Marta va a una reunión con Laura, quien le había prometido tener noticia sobre su posible contrato, ya que lleva 6 meses en la empresa y ha conseguido buenos resultados. Lamentablemente Laura le dice que tendrá que esperar más. Marta queda con Raquel para tomar unas cervezas y conversar un poco:

Raquel: Entonces qué, ¿Fue bien la reunión con tu jefa?

Marta: Hostia que si fue bien, pues no.

Raquel: Habla claro Marta, ¿Qué te dijeron?

Marta: Pues me dijo que me tenía que esperar 3 meses más porque los **cabrones** de recursos humanos tienen que aprobar un presupuesto de no sé qué, ¿Te lo puedes creer?

Raquel: Vaya **chorrada**, ¿Y qué piensas hacer? ¿Buscarás otras opciones?

Marta: De momento quiero relajarme y buscar alguna actividad para reducir el estrés, que estoy por **petar** en cualquier momento.

Raquel: Pues he escuchado que la meditación funciona muy bien para eso, nunca lo he probado pero tengo **colegas** que lo hacen.

Marta: ¿Tú crées? Yo también lo he escuchado, pero no quiero terminar como esos **mataos** que están 2 horas con los ojos cerrados sin hacer nada.

Raquel: Pues mis colegas son un poquillo **frikis** pero muy **majos** también. Además conozco una aplicación que sirve para buscar actividades en grupo como meditación, yoga, baile; tal vez encuentres un grupo **molón.**

Marta: Guay, voy a buscar la app que me dices, a lo mejor me funciona. De momento, ¡Salud! Por 3 meses más jaja.

Raquel: Jaja ¡Salud! Por cierto, ¿Te veré este martes en el gym? Tenemos que quemar estas **cañas** que se acerca el verano.

Marta: Y tanto, ¡Me vas a ver en primera fila!

Raquel: Pues ya veremos.

4. Raquel es una máquina

Marta y Raquel van al mismo gym, y aunque no están apuntadas a las mismas clases siempre intentan juntarse para hacer spinning y conversar un poco.

Durante una sesión de spinning Raquel le cuenta a Marta más detalles sobre el proyecto que le había hablado la última vez:

Raquel: Oye Marta, ¿Te acuerdas que te conté de mi proyecto?

Marta: ¡Claro! ¿Ya me lo puedes revelar o qué?

Raquel: Pues te cuento, no quiero seguir dependiendo de un **puto** jefe que me esté diciendo lo que tengo que hacer, así que he decidido hacerme autónoma.

Marta: **¡Qué dices!** ¡Qué **guay**! ¿Cómo así lo decidiste?

Raquel: La verdad es que no fue fácil pero me di cuenta de que no me gusta trabajar para nadie y creo que puedo tener más libertad si trabajo por mi cuenta.

Marta: Y dime, ¿No tienes miedo? Ser autónomo está bien pero, ¿También es un poco inseguro no?

Raquel: ¡**Total**! Pero ahora que he estado en el paro he podido averiguar bien, hasta me he metido en un grupo de autónomos que hacen **quedadas** cada jueves para ayudarse entre sí. La **peña** es muy **maja** así que creo que todo saldrá bien. Además he podido ahorrar algo estos últimos 3 años así que si pasa algo siempre puedo regresar a trabajar en una empresa.

Marta: ¡**Qué máquina**! Pues, ¡**Dale caña tía**!

Raquel: Gracias, oye te iba a preguntar, ¿Pudiste usar la app que te dije?

Marta: Sí, de hecho encontré un grupo de meditación que hace sesiones los sábados en el Parc de la Ciutadella, voy a ir este **finde**.

Raquel: Seguro que te va a **molar tía**.

Marta: Ya te diré.

5. Unos frikis muy majos

Marta va el sábado por la mañana al Parc de Ciutadella, lugar donde se junta normalmente el grupo de meditación. Al final de la sesión Marta se queda conversando con un chico del grupo:

Marta: Hola, soy Marta. ¡Un placer!

Luís: Hola Marta soy Luís, ¿Qué tal tu primera sesión de meditación?

Marta: Pues está muy **chulo** la verdad. No esperaba que me guste tanto. Lo hacéis todos los sábados, ¿Verdad?

Luís: Sí somos un grupo bastante variado. Aquí viene gente de todas las edades y orígenes.

Marta: Así parece, ¿Tú de dónde eres? Tienes un acento medio raro jaja.

Luís: Jaja, pues yo soy de Colombia, llevo 4 años en Barcelona pero aún no pierdo el acento. ¿Tú de dónde eres y qué te trajo a Barcelona?

Marta: Pues yo soy de un pueblo de Galicia, vine aquí a estudiar un posgrado en contabilidad y ahora hago prácticas en una empresa grande de auditoría pero, ¿Ya sabes qué significa ser becario no? Explotación total, por eso vengo aquí para matar las malas vibras jaja... Por cierto, **¡Qué fuerte** que seas de Colombia! Justo ayer estaba viendo un documental sobre la conservación de los bosques amazónicos en Colombia, ¡Tu país es **una pasada!** ¿Tú que haces aquí?

Luís: Creo que todos estamos aquí para mejorar las vibras jaja... Tienes razón, es un país muy **guapo**, pero es **flipante** lo rápido que se está deteriorando el ambiente, en pocos años no quedará nada, enfin ya sabes lo **capullos** que son los políticos, lo único que les interesa es la **pasta**. Yo trabajo en una ONG para la defensa de los animales.

Marta: ¡Qué interesante! Pues es verdad que sóis un grupo bastante variado. Antes de apuntarme creía que erais todos unos **frikis** jaja.

Luís: Jaja tal vez haya uno que otro, pero somos

gente **guay.**

Marta: ¡Ya lo veo! Tengo que regresar la semana que viene, porque esto **me sienta muy bien**.

Luís: A ver si nos vemos la semana que viene. ¡Que vaya bien!

Marta: ¡Igualmente!

6. No tan mal después de todo

El domingo cenando con Raquel, Marta le cuenta lo divertido que le pareció el meetup. Le cuenta que está muy contenta y que cree que la meditación le va a ayudar mucho a tratar la ansiedad, además de conocer gente que piense como ella.

Raquel: Tía, cuéntame: ¿Qué tal te fue en la meditación?

Marta: La meditación es **una pasada**, antes de comenzar la sesión tenía una **mala leche que no veas** y al terminar salí enamorada de todo jaja.

Raquel: ¡Qué fuerte! ¿Estuvisteis mucho tiempo?

Marta: Pues una horita o así, la verdad es que el lugar no fue el mejor porque a veces había un poco de ruido, pero **nos apañamos**.

Raquel: ¿Y qué tal el grupo, era gente **guay**?

Marta: Sí, era un grupo muy variado. De hecho conocí a un chico de Colombia que trabaja en una ONG para la defensa de los animales. ¿Puedes creer que justo ayer estaba viendo un documental sobre una ONG en Colombia?

Raquel: ¡**Qué heavy**! A lo mejor es el destino jaja... nunca se sabe.

Marta: Pues era un destino bastante guapo eh.

Raquel: Jaja ¿Entonces te ayudó un poco a cambiar ese ánimo?

Marta: La verdad que sí, **me la suda** la empresa, no vale la pena estresarse por **chorradas**. Intentaré ir a la meditación cada sábado.

Raquel: Pues **cojonudo**, me alegra que estés mejor.

• • •

What should have been a week full of positive vibes becomes an eternal suffering for Marta. Her boss Laura doesn't stop harassing her with more work and a treatment that Marta considers unfair. They make her work up to 10 hours every day, plus she's had very little sleep because of the anxiety. Marta can no longer cope with this situation so on Wednesday morning she makes a decision that will change her life forever...

• • •

7. Marta se mete en un marrón

Marta vuelve del curro a las 9 de la noche y se encuentra con Raquel en el salón quien nota la cara de preocupación en Marta, es obvio que algo no anda bien:

Raquel: Oye Marta no te ves muy bien, estás pálida. ¿Te pasa algo?

Marta: Pues nada fuera de lo común... renuncié.

Raquel: ¡Qué dices! ¿Es **coña**?

Marta: No, ya no soporto a Laura, es un **coñazo** trabajar con alguien tan **gilipollas** como ella. Además trabajo **un huevo de** horas y ni siquiera me quieren contratar los **pringados**.

Raquel: Pero parecía que te lo ibas a tomar con calma, ¿no?

Marta: Sí pero estos últimos días han sido terribles, hasta he tenido pesadillas **tía**.

Raquel: Joder, y entonces, ¿Qué piensas hacer?

Marta: No lo sé la verdad, creo que **la he cagado**. Soy becaria así que no cobraré el paro, además la **pasta** me alcanza para dos meses más.

Raquel: ¿Has pensado en pedirle ayuda a tus padres?

Marta: No voy a hacerlo, vine a Barcelona a independizarse no quiero pedirle ayuda a mis padres ni regresar a Galicia.

Raquel: No seas tan **cabeza dura tía**, que los padres están para algo.

Marta: Por el momento no lo haré. No sé si me he metido en un **marrón**, lo único que sé es que no quiero **currar** más en esa empresa.

Raquel: Pues si no estabas contenta trabajando ahí has tomado la decisión correcta.

Marta: Mañana tengo una reunión con Laura, a ver con qué más me sale esta **tía**.

8. Vaya Laura

El jueves Marta va a hablar con su jefa para comentarle que se irá dentro de dos semanas. Su jefa le dice que tendrá que trabajar incluso más para cerrar todos los proyectos que llevaba:

Marta: Buenos días Laura.

Laura: Buenos días, ¿Estás segura de la decisión que has tomado?

Marta: Sí, ya pensé en el preaviso que daré a la empresa. Me iré en dos semanas.

Laura: ¿Dos semanas? Pues eso es muy poco, ¿No crees?

Marta: Es el mínimo por ley, así que me voy en dos semanas.

Laura: ¿Tú si que tienes **cojones** de irte así no?

Marta: No quiero seguir ni un minuto más aquí. Doy 2 semanas de preaviso porque es lo mínimo, sino ya me hubiera **pirado**.

Laura: ¿Sabes que aún tienes **mogollón** de trabajo por hacer no? Vas a estar **a tope** con los proyectos, y los vas a tener que terminar todos.

Marta: Haré los que pueda, no me puedes obligar a quedarme más tiempo aquí.

Laura: Pues te esperan dos semanas muy divertidas.

9. Marta se encabrona

Los nervios de Marta no dan para más, cada día duerme peor y además tiene que aguantar a Carlos, quien dejó los platos sucios otra vez; y además comió un queso que le había enviado su madre de Galicia. Marta **se encabrona** con Carlos:

Marta: ¡Oye Carlos ven aquí!

Carlos: ¿Qué pasa?

Marta: Tú has **pillado** el queso que estaba aquí, está por la mitad.

Carlos: ¿Era tuyo? Pensé que lo había traído un **colega** el sábado que hicimos **botellón**.

Marta: Claro que era mío, es un queso que me envió mi madre de Galicia. Estoy por **darte una buena hostia**.

Carlos: Bueno **no te rayes**, que todavía queda la mitad.

Marta: Cómo quieres que no **me raye** si haces **lo que te sale de los huevos** y encima eres un **guarro**, siempre dejas los platos sucios del día anterior.

Carlos: ¿Y si no te gusta por qué no te **piras** del piso? Nos harías un favor a todos.

Marta: Escucha niño **pijo**, a mí no me hables así, que si pudiera me hubiera ido hace mucho tiempo.

Carlos: Pues nos **montaremos** una buena **farra** ese día **que no veas**.

Marta: Mira, solo no cojas mis cosas y punto.

10. Los papeleos de siempre

El martes Raquel y Marta quedan para hacer spinning juntas y conversar un poco. Esta vez es Raquel quien está muy frustrada porque los trámites para ser autónomo le están tomando mucho tiempo:

Raquel: Tía, no sabes lo **bien que me sienta** un poco de ejercicio al final del día.

Marta: ¡**Total tía,** a mí también! Por cierto, ¿Cómo va eso de ser autónoma?

Raquel: Pues la verdad es que acabo un poco **hasta la polla**. Llevo 4 días esperando que me den cita y estos **tíos** no **espabilan**.

Marta: Ostras, ¿Y no lo puedes hacer por vía telemática?

Raquel: De hecho comencé el trámite por la

web pero es tan **cutre** que me da error cada vez que quiero enviar la solicitud de cita. ¡Estoy **cabreada tía**! Y encima tengo clientes que están esperando.

Marta: Bueno **no pasa nada**, ya sabes que **cabrearse** no va a ayudar. A lo mejor deberías de probar con otro ordenador, muchas veces ese puede ser el problema.

Raquel: Puede ser, ¿Me dejas el tuyo para probar?

Marta: Y tanto, al volver a casa te lo dejo y pruebas.

Raquel: ¡**Guay**!

11. Lana de alpaca pija

Fue una semana intensa para Marta, quien no ve solución a su problema y piensa en todo lo que podría pasar en dos semanas: ¿Encontrará nuevo trabajo? ¿Regresará a Galicia? ¿Tendrá suficiente para vivir?. Son demasiadas preguntas que no la dejan en paz. Marta necesita distraerse así que le propone a Raquel de visitar un mercadillo de artesanía el viernes por la tarde, ya que ambas comparten un gusto por las cosas hechas a mano:

Raquel: ¡Mira ese bolso tan **chulo**! ¿De qué estará hecho?

Marta: Pues **tiene pinta** de ser lana, pero no sé de qué animal… ¡Perdona! ¿Esto es lana verdad?

Vendedor: Sí, es lana de alpaca bebé… viene de Perú.

Marta: Está muy **chulo** y, ¿Cuánto cuesta?

Vendedor: Este de aquí 40 euros.

Marta: ¿40 euros? ¿Pues parece que es lana de alpaca **pija** no? Jaja… Gracias.

Raquel: Jaja alpaca pija, tú sí que estás **chalada**…

Marta: Pues la verdad es que el bolso estaba muy guapo pero 40 **pavos** es un **pastón**, demasiado para una **becaria** que no tiene ni **un duro**.

Raquel: Dios, lo había olvidado, ¿Ya has pensado qué hacer?

Marta: La verdad es que no lo sé… estoy confundida **que te cagas**, tal vez sí me iban a contratar en 3 meses pero no tuve paciencia. ¿Tal vez sea hora de regresar a Galicia?. Hace mucho que no veo a mi familia.

Raquel: Tú sabrás. Me contaste que la meditación te había ayudado, ¿Has vuelto?

Marta: Tienes razón, meditar ese día me **sentó muy bien**. Tengo que regresar este sábado.

Raquel: Ya me dirás si encuentras otro colombiano guapo y salimos los cuatro jaja.

Marta: ¡Dalo por hecho! Jaja.

12. El Luís es muy majo

Marta vuelve a la meditación del sábado con la esperanza de que le ayude a manejar su ansiedad, allí se encuentra con Luís, con quien habla un poco al final de la sesión:

Luís: ¿Qué tal Marta, cómo ha ido la semana?

Marta: ¡Hola Luís! Pues la verdad es que ha sido una semana **chunga,** por eso me tienes aquí jaja.

Luís: ¿Qué ha pasado? Si se puede saber claro.

Marta: Pues para no hacer la historia tan larga mi jefa está **chalada** y me marcho de la empresa en una semana, así que aquí me tienes.

Luís: Jolín, **¡Qué fuerte!** ¿Y sabes qué harás luego?

Marta: No lo tengo muy claro del todo, no

quiero estar en el mismo sector pero no creo que consiga algo en lo que me **mola** que es el desarrollo sostenible.

Luís: ¡**Hostia**! No me habías dicho que te gustaba ese tema, sé de una startup de energía renovable que se llama Bioenergy, están creciendo mucho y necesitan perfiles jóvenes para desarrollar el negocio, a lo mejor te pueda interesar. Un colega mío trabaja ahí y me cuenta que el ambiente laboral **es una pasada**.

Marta: ¿En serio? Pero crees que se puedan interesar en mi perfil, la verdad es que sólo he estado un año de becaria en auditoría y no tengo mucha experiencia.

Luís: Son una empresa bastante moderna y por lo que me dijo mi **colega** son de mente abierta, buscan gente realmente apasionada por el tema, sin importar la industria de la que vengan, así que creo que puede ser una buena oportunidad. Si quieres le paso tu contacto a mi colega, así los de recursos humanos ven tu perfil.

Marta: Sería genial, ¡Qué **majo**!

Luís: Sin problema, ya me contarás.

13. Me puse de los nervios

Marta está muy entusiasmada por la oportunidad que se le ha presentado, aunque todavía tiene dudas sobre si su perfil es el adecuado para el puesto. El miércoles por la mañana tuvo una primera entrevista telefónica con la empresa. Marta no salió con una buena sensación de la entrevista así que se lo cuenta a Raquel para conocer su opinión:

Marta: Raquel **tía**, ¿Te puedo preguntar algo?

Raquel: Claro, dime.

Marta: Pues esta mañana tuve una llamada con la empresa que me recomendó Luís.

Raquel: Jolín es verdad, ¿Qué tal te fue?

Marta: La verdad es que **me puse de los nervios**, felizmente no me hicieron preguntas muy **chungas**. ¿Tú crees que al verme nerviosa se **echen para atrás**?

Raquel: ¡**Qué dices tía**! Todos nos ponemos nerviosos en las entrevistas, eso es normal. Lo importante es que les demuestres lo que vales.

Marta: Tienes razón, tengo que pensar más en positivo.

Raquel: ¡**Total**! Finalmente, ¿Les has contado a tus padres de todo esto? Tal vez te puedan **dar una mano**.

Marta: No les he dicho y no les pienso decir, esta **movida** la quiero resolver por mi cuenta, no les quiero preocupar ni que estén pendientes de mí como si fuera una **chavalilla** de 10 años.

Raquel: A ver, no tienes que ser tan orgullosa eh. Enfin, te tengo que contar algo, pero tiene que ser con un vermut!

Marta: Venga, espero que sea algo bueno.

Raquel: ¡**Y tanto**, ya verás!

14. Fin del papeleo

Raquel y Marta van a una vermutería del barrio. Allí le cuenta las noticias sobre su proyecto de ser autónoma:

Marta: Bueno **chavala**, cuéntame de una vez que me tienes con la intriga.

Raquel: ¿Recuerdas el **papeleo** que tenía que hacer para darme de alta de autónoma?

Marta: Claro, recuerdo que te tenía muy **cabreada**.

Raquel: ¡Pues adivina qué! ¡Ya soy autónoma!

Marta: ¡**Joder**, no te creo!

Raquel: ¡Sí! La verdad es que fue un **lío** tremendo pero finalmente pude presentar todos los papeles. ¡Ahora a **currar**!

Marta: Ahora se viene lo bueno, ¿Me dijiste que ya tenías clientes potenciales no?

Raquel: Sí, de hecho ya he comenzado a montar la estrategia de marketing de un conocido este finde.

Marta: No sabes cuánto me alegro **tía**, te lo mereces.

Raquel: Gracias tía. ¿Y tú me habías dicho que te daban una respuesta esta semana?

Marta: Sí, quedaron en eso. A ver si tengo suerte.

Raquel: Te llamarán, ya verás. ¡Tú eres una **crack**!

Marta: Eso espero jaja.

15. Todo va a salir de lujo

El lunes Marta recibe una llamada sorpresiva de la empresa de energía renovable con la que había tenido una entrevista previamente. Parece que son buenas noticias, así que busca a Raquel, quien está cenando en el salón del piso. No puede contener su alegría y sorpresa:

Marta: Raquel... **tía**, ¡No sabes!

Raquel: ¡Qué pasa! ¡Cuéntame!

Marta: Que me llamaron de la empresa de energía renovable, les gustó mi perfil y quieren que tenga una entrevista con la que sería mi jefa.

Raquel: Jolín, ¡**De puta madre tía**! ¿Y cuándo tendrías esta entrevista?

Marta: Es este miércoles, ¡Ya hasta estoy nerviosa puedes creerlo?

Raquel: Tú **eres la hostia**, ya verás que te van a escoger a ti.

Marta: ¿Cómo crees que me debería de preparar?

Raquel: Pues supongo que te preguntará sobre tu motivación por el puesto y ciertos conocimientos de la industria.

Marta: Tienes razón. A ver si no me pongo nerviosa como la última vez.

Raquel: Tranqui, prepárate bien y vas a ver que todo va a salir **de lujo**.

Marta: Sí, me lo voy a **currar** bien esta vez. Espera… creo que suena mi móvil…

16. La pava de Laura otra vez

Marta va a contestar su móvil a su habitación. Es Laura, quien en un giro inesperado le comenta que los de recursos humanos han conseguido agilizar el proceso de contratación. Para Marta es obvio que no pudieron encontrar a alguien que la reemplace en tan poco tiempo, sin embargo Laura le dice que hay alguien más interesado en el puesto:

Raquel: ¿Era tu móvil?

Marta: Tía esto es el colmo.

Raquel: Joder macho, ¡Y ahora qué pasó!

Marta: Pues me acaba de llamar **pava** de mi jefa. Me dijo que los de recursos humanos agilizaron el proceso para contratarme y me han hecho una oferta. ¿Puedes creerlo?

Raquel: Hostia, **¡Qué fuerte**! ¿Y vas a aceptar?

Marta: Pues les dije que lo tenía que pensar y me dieron hasta el viernes para darles una respuesta.

Raquel: ¿Pensarlo? Pero si era lo que querías, ¿no?

Marta: En principio sí, pero la verdad es que estoy cansada de esa empresa y la otra oportunidad me gusta mucho más, creo que realmente me veo trabajando ahí, no tendría de jefa a una **chalada**, ¿Sabes?

Raquel: ¿Entonces esperarás hasta el viernes?

Marta: Sí, pero también estoy un poco **rayada** porque me dijeron que había otro candidato que estaría interesado en esa posición si yo no les confirmo hasta el viernes. ¿Crees que sea verdad?

Raquel: Joder, sí que son **gilipollas** estos **tíos**, ¿Además de tratarte mal te quieren meter presión de esa forma? La verdad no creo que sea cierto pero nunca se sabe.

17. Flipando con el nuevo proyecto

El miércoles Marta va a la entrevista con quien sería su jefa. Queda enamorada del proyecto. Le dicen que le darán una respuesta a más tardar el lunes de la próxima semana. Marta se encuentra con Raquel en el gym y le cuenta lo sucedido:

Raquel: Marta, ¿Cómo ha ido el día? ¿No era hoy que tenías la entrevista con la nueva empresa?

Marta: Sí, estoy **flipando** con el proyecto, es todo lo que he querido y además tendría la posibilidad de viajar a Sudamérica porque también tienen proyectos allí. Y Carmen, la que sería mi jefa es todo lo contrario a Laura, muy **tranqui**, mentalidad zen. Me encanta porque no me hizo ninguna pregunta **chunga**, sólo se enfocó en entender mi motivación para trabajar ahí. ¿Eso me da muy buena vibra, sabes lo que te quiero decir?

Raquel: Si es lo que te digo, las empresas cada vez se están inclinando a contratar por habilidades blandas, los conocimientos técnicos se pueden aprender en internet o cursos aparte.

Marta: ¡**Total tía**! Aunque hay algo que me preocupa: Me han dicho que me darán una respuesta el lunes y yo tengo hasta el viernes para decidir si aceptar el contrato de mi actual empresa o no.

Raquel: Joder, es verdad. ¿Y entonces qué harás?

Marta: Pues creo que me dejaré llevar por mi instinto y rechazaré la oferta de Laura. No me sentiría bien trabajando más tiempo ahí. Has visto lo nerviosa que me pone esto, ¿No?

Raquel: Es verdad. Y hablando de nervios, no creo que te guste escuchar esto pero el **pavo** del Carlos se ha dejado los platos sucios de nuevo. No lo he visto en todo el día.

Marta: Ya, a estas alturas **me la suda**… tengo cosas más importantes en qué pensar la verdad.

18. Marta sí que va a saco

Luego de haber vencido el plazo para aceptar el contrato de su anterior empresa Marta lo rechaza. Ahora sólo le queda que la acepten en la empresa de energía renovable, quienes se suponen que la llamarán el lunes. El fin de semana se hace interminable. Marta va de nuevo a la meditación del sábado porque lo necesita ahora más que nunca. Ahí se encuentra con Luís con quien se pone al día:

Luís: ¡Qué tal Marta! Cuéntame, ¿Pudiste hablar con los de Bioenergy?

Marta: ¿Cómo va Luís? Pues sí, de hecho tuve un par de entrevistas con ellos y están por darme una respuesta este lunes.

Luís: ¡No me digas! ¡Tú sí que vas **a saco** eh! ¿Y qué tal te pareció el proyecto?

Marta: Me pareció **chulísimo**; y Carmen, la que sería mi jefa es **majísima**.

Luís: Hostia, no sabes cómo me alegra, seguro que te llaman pronto.

Marta: Ya, ojalá porque no me queda de otra la verdad.

Luís: Ya vas a ver que todo va a salir bien. Por cierto, ¿Te gustaría venir a cenar hoy con unos **compis** míos? Hemos visto un **chiringuito** que han abierto hace poco, parece **chulo,** ponen buena música y ofrecen **chupitos** gratis.

Marta: ¡Ah! Creo que ya sé de cuál me hablas. Esta noche no tengo planes así que **guay**, podéis contar conmigo. ¿Sobre qué hora os juntáis?

Luís: Sobre las 8 en la parada del metro de Poblenou.

Marta: Venga, perfecto. ¡Te veo más tarde!

Luís: ¡Hasta ahora!

19. Noche de cotilleo

Marta y Raquel van a cenar a un restaurante vegetariano el domingo por la noche. Ahí charlan un poco sobre el finde:

Raquel: Entonces Marta, cuéntame, ¿Hiciste algo divertido el **finde**?

Marta: ¡Super divertido! Luís me invitó a cenar con unos **compis** suyos a un **chiringuito** de la playa, luego fuimos por unos **chupitos** a un bar muy **guay** que quedaba cerca.

Raquel: ¡Qué **guay**! ¿Y no fuisteis a bailar después?

Marta: Sí, pero todas las discotecas estaban **petadas** de gente así que fuimos a un bar donde también se podía bailar. No te imaginas lo **ciegos** que acabamos, y encima me pedí dos **cubatas** en el bar.

Raquel: ¿Y os **liásteis** o qué?

Marta: ¡**Qué va**! No **nos liamos**, solo lo veo como un amigo. De hecho creo que tiene una **churri** por ahí, así que **ni de coña**. Pero la verdad es que **se nos fue la olla** con los **chupitos** jaja...

Raquel: Jolín, pues yo no terminé mejor. Salí con el grupo de autónomos a un karaoke, no te imaginas el **cebollazo** que **pillé**.

Marta: Madre mía, esto tiene que parar ya jaja.

Raquel: Jaja ¡**Ya te digo tía**!

20. No me llaman, qué putada

Pasan lunes y martes, y Marta aún no recibe respuesta de la nueva empresa. Marta duda mucho si tomó la decisión correcta, siente que ha perdido una gran oportunidad para conseguir el contrato que quería. Ahora está dudando si llamar a sus padres para que la ayuden con todo esto, la ansiedad la mata. El martes por la noche se encuentra con Raquel en el salón del piso, así que habla un poco con ella:

Marta: Tía no me llaman, ¿Qué habrá pasado?

Raquel: Qué **putada tía**, pero te dijeron que te llamarían el lunes sí o sí, ¿Verdad?

Marta: Sí, me dijeron que me darían una respuesta el lunes pero no me han llamado ni enviado ningún correo. ¿Tú crees que haya pasado algo? Tal vez encontraron a alguien mejor para el puesto.

Raquel: No digas **gilipolleces** Marta, lo más probable es que no hayan tenido tiempo de tomar una decisión, después de todo ha pasado muy poco tiempo desde la última entrevista, ¿No?

Marta: Puede que tengas razón. ¿Crees que les debería de llamar para saber una respuesta?

Raquel: Diría que todavía es muy temprano. Estoy segura que no han tenido suficiente tiempo.

Marta: Tienes razón, voy a esperar un poco más.

• • •

Once again Marta falls into anxiety, sleeps very little and can't get out of a loop of negative thoughts. Did they find someone better for the job? Should I go back to my former job? Should I go back to Galicia?. Maybe quitting was a mistake after all...

• • •

21. Todo tiene su final

Es miércoles por la tarde y Marta aún no recibe respuesta. Ahora está pensando si realmente tomó la decisión correcta, ya que lo que estaba buscando en principio era que la contratasen, y finalmente le ofrecieron un contrato. Ahora Marta tiene sentimientos encontrados y está considerando escribirle a su actual jefa para preguntarle si aún tiene una posibilidad de ser contratada después de haber rechazado la oferta, pero justo en ese momento recibe una llamada de un número desconocido:

Interlocutor: Hola, ¿Hablo con Marta? Habla Montse de Bioenergy.

Marta: Sí habla ella.

Montse: Pues te quería hablar con respecto a tu candidatura para el puesto de ventas en Bioenergy, ¿Tienes unos minutos?

Marta: Claro, cuéntame.

Montse: Primero disculparme porque en principio habíamos quedado en hablarte el lunes pero quien llevaba tu candidatura está de baja y yo he tenido que retomar tu candidatura. Por otro lado me gustaría decirte que nos ha gustado mucho tu perfil y queremos hacerte una oferta bajo las condiciones que habíais acordado inicialmente.

Marta: Jolín, ¡Qué alegría! Me parece perfecto.

Montse: Dime, ¿Cuándo te vendría bien comenzar?

Marta: Pues mi pre-aviso terminó el viernes, así que estoy libre para comenzar cuando vosotros creáis mejor.

Montse: Perfecto, ¿Podrías venir mañana a la oficina a firmar el contrato?

Marta: Sí, mañana me va bien.

Montse: Pues te veo mañana Marta, hasta entonces.

Marta: ¡Hasta mañana Montse!

FIN

• • •

Although the initial goal of this story is for you to learn the use of slang words and expressions in colloquial Spanish, we also wanted to send a message: If you listen to your heart and follow your intuition you will find the real path to happiness, even if the odds are against you.

• • •

THANKS FOR READING!

Every minute spent writing this book has been a pleasure because I know it will help you build new relationships, which at the end is the goal of learning any language. And we won't end up here, we'll continue working on better tools based on your needs, that's why we'd kindly ask you to leave your honest review on this book. To do this you just need to go to your Amazon account and search for this book at the 'Your orders' section.

I hope you enjoyed and learned a lot from this book, and if you have any questions or suggestions just hit us up at contact@digitalpolyglot.com. It will be our pleasure to help you in any inquiry you have.

I wish you a wonderful day!

Alejandro from Digital Polyglot.

About Digital Polyglot

Digital Polyglot was born in 2015 with one clear mission: Inspire you to break down language barriers, spreading understanding among people from different cultures and softening the rough edges of any kind of inequality.

With this mission in mind we're constantly creating language-learning related content on our blog and eBooks like this one.

Make sure to follow us on Facebook and Instagram for more fun language content!

Join the club!

Are you looking for more words and expressions to further enrich your vocabulary? Maybe you wanna know more about the origin of each word? Perhaps you are curious about what happened to Marta after she got hired?. To get more exclusive content for Spanish and other languages make sure to join the club supporting us at Patreon: patreon.com/digitalpolyglot. This will help us bring you more and better resources to take your language skills to the next level!

As a Patreon member you will have exclusive access to:

- A bunch of more words and expressions that were not mentioned in this eBook.
- Words classified by level of vulgarity and frequency of use.
- Regional classification of words, since not all words are used everywhere.
- Even more conversations so you practice each

word in an informal context.

With a small contribution starting at 5$/ month you will be able to improve your level of Spanish, and you will help us improve the quality of our content.

Let the journey begin!

Printed in Great Britain
by Amazon

35396028R00098